A

Cut on broken line

Cut on broken line

Tang Dynasty
618–907

Plate 1

Tang Dynasty
618–907

Plate 2

Song Dynasty
960–1279

Plate 3

Song Dynasty
960–1279

Plate 4

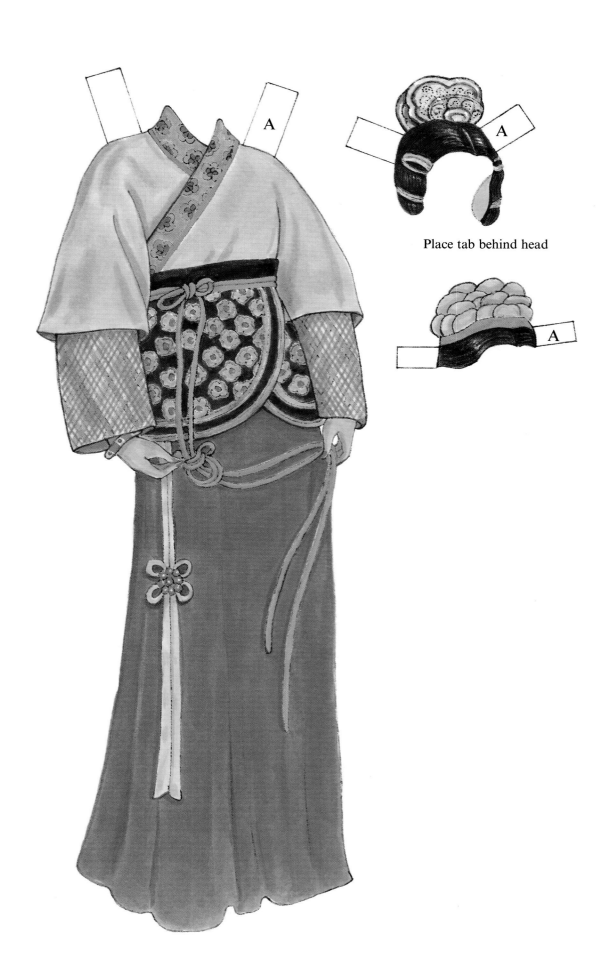

Place tab behind head

Yuan Dynasty
1279–1368

Plate 5

Yuan Dynasty
1279–1368

Plate 6

Yuan Dynasty
1279–1368

Plate 6

Place tab behind head

A

Ming Dynasty
1368–1644

Plate 7

Ming Dynasty
1368–1644

Plate 8

A

Place tab behind head

Qing Dynasty
1644–1911

Plate 9

Qing Dynasty
1644–1911

Plate 10

Place tab behind head

Qing Dynasty
1644–1911

Plate 11

Place tabs behind head

Qing Dynasty
1644–1911

Plate 12

Place tab behind head

Republic Period
1911–1949

Plate 13

Plate 14

Republic Period
1911–1949

Place tab behind head

Republic Period
1911–1949

Plate 15

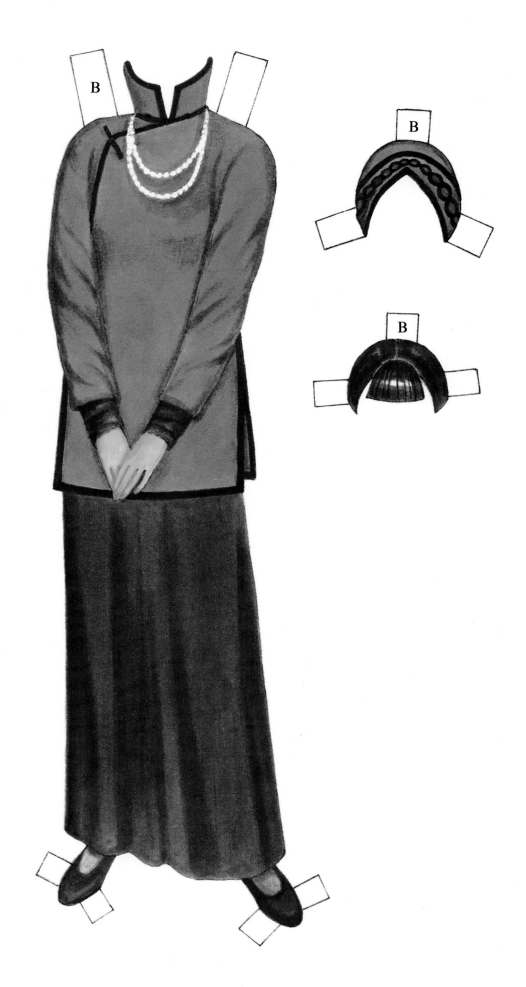

Republic Period
1911–1949

Plate 16